4490 W. Reformatory Rd

Pennelton Indiana

46064

Sheree Bledsoe

go to 169 N
Exit 37B

Take IN 38 W exit
Exit 219
toward Pendleton

Victoria's Goals

11/1/2015 SB

11/2015 Laptop

2015/11 – 11/30: Stay in school

2015/12 – 12/1: find a Job

1/2016: Go back to school

4/2016: Spring breck → PARTY / Prom / Florida

5/2016: Graduation Yay PARTY

8/2016: Police Academy – College

This is a **FLAME TREE NOTEBOOK**

Yin and Yang • ISBN 978-1-78361-142-3

FLAME TREE PUBLISHING LIMITED
Crabtree Hall, Crabtree Lane, London SW6 6TY, United Kingdom
www.flametreepublishing.com